Praise for This Book!

"A life-changing book with a life changing message. Talk Less, Pray More is a must read for anyone desiring a closer walk with God. Lesa Day's transparency to share her personal walk with God is both inspiring and empowering to all who read it. Lesa takes the reader along with her on a spiritual journey, as she shares priceless lessons that can only be learned when a child of God talks less and prays more."

~ Dion Jordan, The Potentialist, author *of All That It Takes Is All That You've Got And All That You've Got Is All It Takes"*

"This book written by God, through Lesa Day is a significant reminder to us all. Within the pages of this magnificent book is a profound message of listening and walking in love. This great love will guide us around every obstacle in life as long as we listen and hold on to it."

~ Anthony Goulet, author of *God Help Me Tie My Shoes & The Four*

"I must say this book caused me to take a good look at my attitude toward prayer and what God has been trying to tell me. The stories and their connection to God's word really rang true for me. The chapter on forgiveness was so on point and spoke to me directly, causing me to miss boarding my plane because I was focused on what God was saying to me. This book was worth missing my flight, so I could finish it. Great reading, great testimony Lesa Day...thank you for sharing your story."

~ Mark Wiggins, The Speaker Man, author of *Permission to Succeed & Mapping Your Journey to Success*

"This book is a beautiful writing of one woman's journey to intimacy with God, growing deeper in trust of the ONE she loves, her Lord, her Creator! It was a blessing to take the journey with Lesa Day, as God calls her from a place of brokenness, from complacency into a walk of surrender...to a place she had never known before. Thank you Lesa! Through the sharing of your own journey and the questions in each chapter, you show us how to consider our own walk with God."

~ Theresa Robbins, Youth Group Leader

Talk Less

Pray More

God Said: Be Quiet & Pray

By

Lesa Day

Carol,
Pray More ♥♥
Lesa Day
cm

Talk Less, Pray More by Lesa Day

Printed in the United States of America.
All right reserved.
ISBN: 978-0-615-92360-4

Printed by
We Win Publishing
204 Eagle Court
Springfield, Georgia 31329
www.pray-more.com

Dedication

To all of the prayer warriors, who have stood in the gap for God's kingdom in the past, and will do so for present and future generations.

Table of Contents

I Walked Down a Dirt Road
with Jesus

*I resisted the call for some time. Yet through
His love and patience the Lord prepared me
for such a time as this.*

The dream happened more than a decade ago. One afternoon I laid down for a nap and was half asleep when images appeared and the movie-like dream began. I walked with Jesus down a dusty road. To our right was thick, well-trimmed grass and beyond was a dark-blue river of white caps. Mature oak trees were scattered throughout the grassy area and others stood as sentinels of shade along the river. To our left was a field of tall, tulip-shaped flowers. The multi-hued flowers of bright highlight-yellow, deep rich violet, magenta and royal blue swayed in the breeze. Jesus was holding my left hand as we walked down the road. He seemed much taller than me.

He was wearing a white tunic and sandals. His hair fell just past his shoulders, and Light emanated from Him and surrounded his upper body. His light was bright, but soft on my eyes so I could see Him. All I could feel was love and peace. The love flowing from Him overwhelmed me so that speaking didn't seem possible or even necessary. I never let go of His hand.

We continued down the road and saw there were rocks along the center. The rocks were not easily noticed, as their brownish-ochre colors blended in to the road. The rocks were smooth and round, sort of like a large turtle shell. We would have tripped had we not noticed the rocky earth. As we walked down the road for some distance, each time we came upon a rock, Jesus steered me around it. Although no words were spoken between us, I noted that there was a message for me to receive. Then my eyes opened, and I realized I was dreaming. I closed my eyes again, not wanting to awaken. I wanted to stay there and just continue basking in His presence.

I've had time to meditate on this dream and deepen my walk with God over the years. I've seen my life experiences tie back to this dream, and learned that I have a message to share with you. I believe this dream applies to anyone walking with the Lord. God took me from being a babe in Christ needing milk to an adult ready for meat and willing to surrender my life to Him. (Heb 5:12-14) God showed me the power of prayer, which is a daily commitment to be renewed each morning. God has nurtured, healed, matured, and prepared me with gifts to serve His Kingdom as an intercessor.

As you read, you'll experience this journey too and see how God walked with me to teach me grace, mercy, surrender, and a deeper understanding of His love. In fact, each lesson was like an intense mountain climb. On this walk with Jesus, I faced three mountains. The first was the mountain of grace and mercy, which brought me deeper understanding of deception and disrespect. The second mountain of surrender showed me that talking less and praying more would replace how I ministered to those who came for help. Finally, the third mountain of intercession truly required daily discipline in self-control to learn how I had to move out of God's way...one tough mountain!

The purpose of this book is to share my journey with you in hopes that God draws you closer to Him and reveals a clearer understanding of how the awesome power of prayer can heal, and transform your life. God deeply wants to bring healing and wholeness to His children. He wants to see the body of Christ whole and united to build His kingdom on this earth, and with very good reason.

A spiritual battle is occurring right now around us, and we must decide to take the offense to defeat the enemy. My prayer is that your intimacy with God grows deeper. My desire is that He renews your hope and belief that you have already won any battle that's brought before you.

I provide questions at the end of each chapter to encourage you to pause and seek the Lord to hear His voice. I urge you to use this time to go deeper and purposely seek Him. Willingly allow the Holy Spirit to teach, encourage, and direct you. May you be launched forward to fulfill the call He has for your life and may God be glorified!

Lesa Day, Thanksgiving, 2013

"I am your best Friend, as well as your King. Walk hand in hand with Me through your life. Together we will face whatever each day brings: pleasures, hardships, adventures, disappointments.[i]

Chapter 1

Prayer is a Conversation
and a Battle Cry

Long before I became a Christian, I had a strong belief in prayer. I often prayed to God as a child in my bed ready for a night's sleep and arising in the morning to start a new day. As I dedicated my life to Christ in my early twenties, I easily called out to the Lord even in the smallest matters, because I had done so since childhood. Great mentors came into my life who taught, challenged, and directed me in seeking a strong, intimate relationship with the Lord. I dug into God's Word, came to know Him as my Abba Father (Daddy), and I learned to come boldly to His throne. I prayed to God with expectations for God to move on behalf of His children, whatever their needs might be. After my prayers, I said, "It is finished. Okay, God, now it is your turn to move as You choose. I have come to You in prayer, and now I am released from the situation."

Well, almost! I knew only too well that the mindset *faith without works* was fruitless. After praying, the question always popped into my mind about what could I do to fix this problem. Then answers came too. I had solutions and action steps to get to the end result.

I gave it to God, and then I'd take it back. Can you picture it? Are there instances that come to your mind right now when you brought a situation before God, gave it to Him, and then took it back? This is so easy for me to do because my professional experiences include teaching, coaching, and mentoring.

Yet, in the last four years, God took me on a journey that was about molding me to talk less and pray more. Are you familiar with those teachings about you being the clay and God being the potter who shapes each of us to be more like Christ? At times, how He's given me certain revelations has been hilarious. At other times, the experiences were extremely painful, as He was sculpting me, His clay, and then firing me in the kiln to set the clay correctly and purify me. Each time I gained more clarity.

For example, I can do a lot of talking as a person who comes to teaching naturally. Yes, I am also a good listener, but I am more a natural exhorter. After His nudges, I instantly encouraged people who spoke with me and steered them toward solutions. This season, however, the situation had changed. God has had me in a season I can only describe as the need to put tape over my mouth to talk less and pray more. I'll confess that I've done it kicking and screaming at times. However through His love and grace, I now understand why this is so critical for His glory.

Prayer is…

- A conversation with our Father in heaven.

- The intimate moments of sharing thoughts and feelings.

- Those sweet talks as you consider all that you are grateful for.

- The whispered moments of pain and sadness, in need of comfort and healing.

- You can experience his presence as you walk with Him in the cool of the day or the heat of the battle.

Prayer is also a battle cry when fighting spiritual warfare necessary to defeat the enemy that is seeking to steal, kill, and destroy all of God's people (John 10:10). Prayer is the offensive weapon we have been given to win the battle set before us (Eph. 6:17-18).

Both types of prayer are equally important. One is fulfilling God's greatest desire for intimacy with you. The other allows you to push through the darkness to walk in victory as you obey the call God has given.

In either case Jesus wants to continue to hold your hand as you walk down that dirt road. Will you allow Him to direct you and protect you from obstacles of the enemy? He wants you to see His glory unfold as you walk in obedience and experience the depth of His love.

♥ Reflections

Can you recall times in your life when that sweet period of prayer brought you closer to God? Describe it? *When He puts words in my mouth*

Do you think of God as your Abba Father (Daddy), who is there to comfort, teach and encourage you? How did you learn this? *Protect*

Can you describe seasons in your life that your prayers have been a battle cry to fight spiritual warfare? Explain?

If you take your eyes off Me and follow another's way, you are in grave danger. Even well-meaning friends can lead you astray if you let them usurp My place in your life. The way to stay on the path is to keep your focus on Me. Awareness of My presence is your best protection.[ii]

Chapter 2

I Allowed Idolatry to Sneak into My Life

For over twenty years I have lived my life by this scripture, Here I am, Send me! (Is. 6:8)

Seriously, I've considered myself a modern day missionary living in various cities and states in the U.S. I might be somewhere for a couple of weeks consulting or in a long-term position that lasts six years. I wasn't doing straight up evangelism. My call has been that of teaching and coaching in leadership and character building. My passion has been for people to become intently aware that their lives are a lasting legacy whether they are building a company or parenting the next generation. I provide tools and guidance as the Lord allows me to do so.

This journey had required faith for the Lord's provision in all areas of my life. From the place I slept at night to the finances needed to be without a full time job for months at a time. I've learned to be still and know that He is God (Ps. 46:10 NIV).

Anybody who knows me understands I am a naturally structured person, highly organized, and easily predictable. Adventurous yes, but I plan the adventure rather than spontaneously jumping off the cliff wondering what might happen next. Do you ever notice that when you are truly seeking to serve God He will make do you just the opposite of your natural tendency? That's exactly what has happened in my life.

Instead of allowing me to create and live by a five-year plan, God reminds me He is in control. A choice to surrender one's life to God requires faith and trust. I may think I know how long each assignment or season in my life will last, but in reality He has brought me to an understanding of daily surrender to Him and not to be concerned with tomorrow, for tomorrow will have its own challenges to overcome. (Matt 6:34) As I surrendered He drew me closer and allowed me a much deeper intimacy to experience His presence and hear His voice.

Just before I had the dream of walking down a dirt road with Jesus, I was going through a battle of holding onto a relationship for a couple of years. I had to let go and needed God's help to release me from it. It wasn't a bad relationship, but it was an idol and deterring me from fulfilling the call God had on my life. This was one of the toughest battles I've fought because this man I cared for so deeply would never do anything to deter me from doing God's work. John is one of my greatest encouragers and I could be completely transparent with him. I could trust he wanted what was best for me. I wanted more than friendship. I had never met a man whom I could totally submit to as a husband until I met John. I had matured in my walk with God where I was totally comfortable in my singleness. I was okay with just serving the Lord the rest of my life as a single lady and doing ministry as He called me to do so. When those feelings for John were stirring so deep inside me, I was doing a lot of talking with the Lord about what His will for me would be. When I allowed myself to be completely vulnerable and share my heart with John he was in awe and quite speechless at first. He told me he couldn't see it happening. He explained that he felt my walk with the Lord was far more mature than his, and he couldn't see himself being the head of my household. Truthfully, it deepened my feelings for him even more because it allowed me to trust him. I felt safe and secure that he really wanted what was best for me. I did agree with him that there were definite areas where I was more spiritually mature than him, but I also was aware that no two people are walking exactly the same in their walk with God.

Marriage is supposed to be a spiritual union of two people, who submit themselves to the Lord, and together do the will of the Father for the glory of His kingdom. This involves love, growth, encouragement, disagreements, and trials among many other things that may happen in a lifetime, but it still remains that marriage should glorify God and build His kingdom. I could see this happening with John and me. This was not a situation where it was friends with benefits. This was a pure friendship involving two people walking with the Lord encouraging one another. No physical intimacy or sex of any kind. Abstinence has not been a battle for me. After I poured my heart out to John and listened to his response, my attitude was that I would wait.

If it's God's will He will make it happen. He will transform our hearts and bring us together. While waiting, I relocated to a different city for work upon God's leading. As time went by, I realized I allowed this desire for John to have a strong, emotional hold on me. A soul tie had been created.

Do you have those relationships in your life right now? A soul tie strong enough that you center your life on a specific person? It may not seem that way on the surface.

I went to work, did an excellent job, continued with my day to day tasks and life continued. Then the question came to mind: what if suddenly God asks me to make a significant change in my life? Maybe send me to do missionary work for three years? Or stay open and flexible to living in various different locations to do the work He's called me to do?

I admit my heart's desire at the time was to eventually be back in the same city as John, and I prayed God would bring us together. I hadn't realized how strong an influence this relationship was, until I noticed myself thinking: what would John think? If I did a specific thing how would this affect our relationship in the future? I had allowed the soul connection to John to get so strong that it hindered my willingness to freely say, "Yes God, I'll do whatever You want without considering those what-if questions." I had put John first in my life and God second.

Once I realized this, my heart broke as I went before God in repentance and asked Him for forgiveness. I asked that He give me whatever I needed to break the soul tie and sincerely put God back as first place in my life. I cried before the Lord as I experienced the loss of the relationship. I had to stand in faith that my Father in heaven knew what was best for me. It took a bit of time for God to walk me through this process, for me to truly realize how strong the soul tie was, and how much I had allowed it to control my decisions.

His love and grace are never-ending, as I cried out to Jesus to be set free. I think the letting-go part happened in stages for me. The time came when God knew I was ready to truly let go. He miraculously broke the soul tie instantly and brought me peace. How do I know that? The yearning I had, and the priority of John being first in my life went away.

After that, as John and I spent time together, I could just enjoy the moment and not think about what might be or could be. It didn't matter. I had let go and had been released of the soul tie. John was in my thoughts less and less. Two days after God gave me the breakthrough and released me from the stronghold of the relationship, I took an afternoon nap. I had the dream of walking down the dirt road with Jesus. I had never felt such love, peace, and intimacy with the Lord. It felt like a bit of heaven. The dream was confirmation of my decision to let go of the relationship, and the Lord was now back as first place in the center of my life.

I felt like I let go of the Lord's hand due to the stronghold of the relationship I desired with John. God wanted me to know that no matter the challenges, if I chose to hold His hand, He would walk me through the process around each obstacle, and I could experience His peace. I did not have to fear or be anxious about anything (Phil 4:6).

The big question was would I continue to hold His hand or let go and allow my flesh to be in control to fulfill my desires? I found it interesting in the dream that Jesus was holding my left hand. That would be the hand where a wedding ring would be placed if marriage were God's will for me. It indicated to me that Jesus is my husband as He should be to every single lady serving Him. Jesus is my husband who sees that my every need is fulfilled. He gives me complete peace as I continue to seek Him and walk this journey holding His hand.

As for John and me, John remains one of my best friends to this day, and I would want nothing more than for Him to be happy and fulfill the call God has for his life.

♥ Reflections

What steps are you taking to keep God first in your life? *Adoration - Reading - email, letters & praising Him*

What intimate moments have you experienced with the Lord? *when I recognize that He helped me* 21 *Verbally*

Is prayer an essential part of your relationship with God? *Yes*

Are you holding His hand and letting Him lead you in your daily walk? How do you know? *Not always*

Have you let go of His hand and chosen to make your own path? What does it feel like to you? Are you ready to come back and take His hand?

Jesus I trust in you

"Seek My Face, and you will find all that you have longed for. The deepest yearnings of your heart are for intimacy with Me. I know, because I designed you to desire Me.[iii]

Chapter 3

God's Greatest Desire Is Intimacy with His Children

The dream gave me such clarity of the intimacy He wants with His children.

As I sought the Lord more through prayer, I experienced deeper peace. It became a two-way conversation. As I released my burdens into His hands, I experienced more freedom. My trust increased as I put my faith in Him.

I have had a strong calling for many years to work with families. I assist parents to create a nurturing structure in their home that encourages a strong parent/child connection while developing good character and healthy self-esteem. God has blessed me with a large network of people around the globe. My attitude has always been God you lead the way! You close any door of opportunity that's not Your will for me. I am in awe when I ponder the many times God has allowed me to pour into people's lives. It can happen anywhere. All God asks of me or you is to be willing and attentive to the movement of the Holy Spirit. This has happened on planes as I travel extensively around the country, on trains and buses going into New York City, and by phone as I'm doing my business as usual. People have poured their hearts out to me, seeking prayer and encouragement as the Holy Spirit moved, and I listened to their stories. I've coached engineers in China by phone on leadership and team building that turned into a two-year Bible study with a lady engineer, who was hungry for a relationship with God.

I didn't specifically ask for this, but my heart was willing, and God allowed amazing things to come my way when I've served Him. This increased my faith and experience of His power. God provides amazing gifts that grow your faith. I experience an overflow of gratitude, as God allows me to be His vessel and use my passion to teach and impact others. I am excited to rise each morning whenever these opportunities are brought before me. In this growing intimacy with the Lord, I learned to depend on him for all my needs. My prayers were ongoing throughout the day filled with praise, gratitude, and transparency to the point of whining at times when things weren't going my way.

In my career as a coach, I've authored or coauthored four books, created online classes and have spoken at conferences. As a Type A personality, an achiever, my mindset has been about the next assignment of "doing" work for God. The mindset was never about success or failure, as much as what's the next course of action.

God was about to turn my world upside down. He did it in three stages over a four-year period. It would be necessary for me to continue to hold His hand, or I would trip over the obstacles in the road, and I did. You will see as this story unfolds. Each mountain I climbed made me continuously cling to Him in prayer. He reminded me that His deepest desire is intimacy with His children, as well as to receive the glory He deserves as God of the universe. Henry Blackaby said, "God's invitation to work with Him causes a crisis of belief that requires faith and action."[iv] That action for me was to talk less and pray more.

♥ Reflections

The world is full of distractions. You don't have to walk out your front door with all the gadgets of technology used today. As I sit here writing at my laptop, I could easily open up five others windows to distract me. I have tabs for email, Facebook, LinkedIn, or Twitter. Imagine those people you love so much and are eager to spend time with…maybe your spouse, your child, a brother, sister or a parent? Whoever that person might be, imagine that suddenly they don't have time for you?

Mom, your son is heavily into playing video games and when you try to engage in a conversation, he just sort of grunts out answers as though he doesn't want to be bothered. You can put limits on how much he can play the video games, but, regardless, that's where his heart is at the moment.

Husbands, maybe your wife is heavily involved in women's ministry. She's preoccupied and overwhelmed with managing the home and keeping up with her responsibilities. As her husband, you would like to spend time with her. You feel like she's running around constantly with something to do. She's not stopping for a moment to say, "Hi, how are you doing?"

Ladies, your husband is dealing with a lot of pressure at work. He comes home each night feeling stressed out. He needs more staff but doesn't have the funding to hire more people. His boss is pressuring him to increase production. You reach out by asking him how you can encourage or help him, and he has no answer. He's pulling away because he knows you can't do anything about it, and as a man, he wants to try and figure it out himself. You want to connect with him and spend time with him, but he wants to go into his own cave. He'd rather spend time by himself in front of a ball game or playing golf with his buddies. Do you feel like he's pushed you away?

Do any of these scenarios resonate with you? Is it happening to you right now? Are you lonely? Are you reaching out to someone you love, and he or she isn't recognizing it? It hurts doesn't it?

Now imagine how your Father in heaven feels? In the beginning He created us in His image. He wants us to walk with Him in the cool of the day, like He did with Adam and Eve in the garden. He desires to share a love with you that only He can give you. It is the very reason He created you and me…to have an intimate relationship with God! This personal friendship is so close that no one can separate us from Him. He desires an intimacy that goes far beyond any accomplishment you make during your lifetime on this earth. Distractions come so easily that it's necessary to intentionally stop for a moment to say, "Hey God, what's up?"

Imagine your son becoming a world-renowned scientist, who finds a cure for cancer, and you haven't spoken with him in five years. How does that make you feel? It's painful and lonely isn't it? You love your son and yearn to spend time with him to hear what's happening in his life. You find out what he's doing by reading the headlines of all the global newspapers. As a parent, who loves your son beyond any words, losing that intimate connection with your child is heart wrenching, isn't it?

Imagine how God feels if the very reason He created you was to have a deep, personal relationship, and you walk on by, not giving him a second thought. He sees you succeed, fall, stumble, experience pain, joy, loss, and He wants to be there every step of the way. Yet, He can't if you don't call out to Him, and calling out to Him is done through prayer. Can you feel Him tugging at your heart?

How would you describe your intimacy with God?
On & off – just like all my relationships
Can you imagine Him as your "daddy" who is always there to love you, comfort you, and protect you? Do you also allow Him to be there during those whining and screaming moments?

Can you shift your thinking from God being "Abba Father" (Daddy) to almighty God, who is the creator of the universe and receives the honor and glory for your life? The One who corrects you because He loves you and wants what's best for you?

Spending time alone with me can be a difficult discipline, because it goes against the activity addiction of this age. You may appear to be doing nothing, but actually you are participating in battles going on within spiritual realms. You are waging war – not with the weapons of the world, but with heavenly weapons, which have divine power to diminish strong-holds. Living close to Me is a sure defense against evil. [v]

Chapter 4

I Told God I Wanted to be More Like Jesus

Leadership Through The Back Door

God moved on my time clock for years, or so it seemed. In 1992, leaving my home state was the beginning of my journey to go anywhere God called me to go. I packed my car with only the necessities and headed for Atlanta, Georgia because that is where the doors started to open. I had no idea what I would do when I arrived. Only six months prior, I attended a conference in Tulsa, Oklahoma to seek direction from the Lord; I knew He was about to move me. I looked at five different cities for employment, and every door seemed to be opening in the Atlanta area, but nothing was definite. I drove away in faith and believed God would direct me to the right place.

For the next twelve years, as soon as He closed one door, He would open another. There was no real effort on my part, as it just happened.

Then I started to notice a change, as I networked throughout the country. Opportunities seemed scarce. I felt lost, like I was wandering around and asking God, "So…what's up? Am I doing something wrong here? What do you want me to do?" Yet, He had never left me.

He was right there and continued to give me many opportunities to minister to others. The ministry varied from within my local community to weekly phone calls mentoring women in the Word of God, who lived in other parts of the world. My heart was full of gratitude that God allowed me to be His vessel. On the other hand, I asked Him how I was supposed to support myself with no regular paycheck. He continued to provide my every need, especially in my deep sadness.

A family tragedy happened! I lost my eighteen-year-old brother to a heart attack. This was the second time God had shown me so clearly the desperate need to pray. The night before my brother passed away, I was on the phone interceding with a dear Christian sister, as the Holy Spirit led us to pray. I hadn't felt my brother come up as strongly before, as he did this night. When I received the call the next morning, I continued to hold the hand of Jesus tighter, knowing He would direct me and give me His peace because I was shocked and had no words. Nor did I know what to do.

I flew home to spend time with family and to attend my brother's memorial service. Never had I been so still and quiet while waiting on God's leading. I felt helpless. I couldn't stop the pain of dear family members, whom I loved so much. I did what I could to serve and make their lives a little more comfortable. Two people got saved and accepted Jesus as their personal savior when they came to me for ministry during the tragedy.

I had some serious questions about my brother, as to whether he was saved; I fought this inner battle daily as I cried out to my Father in heaven. Again, God in His amazing love for me brought me comfort and peace on the flight back to Atlanta. I was on my computer writing in my journal, and the pilot made the announcement for landing. As I looked out the window, I saw the longest rainbow I had ever seen. It seemed to wrap around the top of the plane to the bottom. I paused to consider if this was a sign from God.

Later, the following week, I shared the story with my fellowship group, and a dear friend confirmed that rainbow, in fact, was a sign from the Lord. She reminded me that God created the rainbow for Noah, and it was a sign that His promise was fulfilled. She encouraged me not to be concerned and to trust that the Lord had shown me I could let go, knowing my brother was in heaven. I felt God's peace and let go. Oh, how loving and gracious our Father in heaven is to His children.

As I tried to get back to my normal routine I sought and waited for my next work assignment. No doors opened for a couple of months, and then a promising position came up in New York City. I was getting ready to travel and meet with the client in person, and then another family crisis happened that put the job on hold.

My mom had a simple gall bladder removal operation. The night before, as I spent time in prayer, suddenly I got a terrible feeling as my mom came to mind. I knew these sudden thoughts of mom served as a warning that surgery wasn't going to go as smoothly as expected. I went before the Lord interceding for my mom and stood against any hold the enemy may try to have on the situation. As I prayed, the Lord gave me the peace I needed that everything would be all right, and mom would be fine.

Yet, the warning came to pass. Complications happened, and I flew home four days later to be with mom in the hospital. She needed to return for emergency surgery, as one of the ducts opened, and bile from the gall bladder seeped into her body. The second surgery successfully removed all of the toxic bile. Mom was sedated into a semi-coma so she could rest and recover. Otherwise her anxiety level would have lengthened her recovery time. All of the immediate family knew mom never wanted to be left

33

alone in a hospital. Dad would have never left her side had I not been there. I took the night shift and dad took the day shift, and we kept this schedule for five weeks. I sat there by her side night after night, praying, talking with her even though she couldn't respond to me, and meditating as to what God might be showing me. I stood firm on the confirmation God gave me that she would be okay.

Again, God showed me how powerful prayer is when I listen and hear Him for the warning signs, as He did with the loss of my younger brother. How helpless I would have felt had I been working in a full time position and couldn't be at my mother's side during this time. This lesson increased my trust in the Lord. No matter how the circumstances looked on the outside, He was guiding and directing me each step of the way. God knew the things that were going to happen in my family that year and the time I would need to be with family for my own sanity.

As my mom recovered, and I got the release to start seeking work again, I was back to work within two weeks. The same position I considered in New York before my Mom went in for her operation was still available. The Lord kept the door open for two months and gave me more confirmation to trust Him. He had everything under control. His plan was perfect.

I mentioned previously that I sensed a change coming. As a coach, I'm naturally goal oriented. Set a goal, come up with a plan, and bring it to fruition. The Type A personality in me wants to get to the end result as quickly as possible. Let's just get it done!

Spending time in prayer with the Lord started showing me the importance of detours from the goal.

How imperative they are for Him to be able to mold and shape me to become more Christ-like. He reminded me of instances where I was following a plan to reach a certain goal, and then He took me on detours before I attained what I had set out to do. For instance, let's say for simplicity sake, it would take ten action steps to complete the goal. Yet, when I reached step number six, God sent me on a detour for something I hadn't anticipated. My brother's death and my mom's surgery complications were detours I hadn't planned.

Detours have a profound impact when you consider the transformation that occurs during the process. While my mom was in the hospital I experienced the Lord's sweet presence that encompassed me with a peace that no words can explain. I witnessed a love and dedication between my parents that brought tears to my eyes each time I contemplated its depth. A person can't understand this until a trial happens, and God brings you through it. You get to see a person's true character when they are tested during a crisis or setback. I was overwhelmed with gratitude, often to the point of tears, as I experienced the love and dedication of my family during this time.

Another detour occurred that allowed my ministry to expand to China and work with high level government employees on a weekly basis. While I was living in Chicago, a lady approached me in a Bible study and asked me if I'd be willing to help men and women attaining their Master's Degree at the University of Chicago with their English. I accepted the opportunity and had weekly meetings with them. I thought this would be a possibility to minister and plant seeds into people's lives. Fellowship with them blessed me greatly, more so for me than for them.

A year later a friend of mine was expanding a technology business to China and requested that I mentor three of his employees in leadership and time management. Salvation came to one of the ladies, and I did Bible study with her by phone each Friday night for two years. What a detour! Who would have thought I would be doing a weekly Bible study with someone on the other side of the world?

We serve a God, who has a much bigger vision than we have. All we have to say is, "Yes, Lord, I'll go! Yes, Lord, I'll do it!" However, the detours were not part of my ten-step plan to attain certain goals in my life. Instead, the detours were extraordinary opportunities for me to serve the Lord.

For four years people were asking me to write a book about my approach and philosophy when working with families. My response was oh no, I really don't like to write. After mom's surgery, I took the job and moved to New York. I was in a comfortable spot in the woods about an hour north of Manhattan. Truthfully, I had become a city girl, who thoroughly enjoyed the atmosphere and buzz the city had to offer...the museums, live theater, and all the wonderful ethnic foods I loved to taste.

Being out in the woods was a bit boring for this lady, but I knew God called me to be there. As it turned out, the place was perfect for me to write my first book. The Lord gave me a dedicated team of people for the project, and it was published within twelve months.

Yet, I kept sensing those changes in the atmosphere again. This time was about my career. Was I surprised when resistance I hadn't seen before kicked in! I'm looking to God and asking, "What's up? Am I doing something wrong?" Little did I know that God was calling me to intercede more in prayer versus the teaching I normally did when working with clients. My methods worked repeatedly, so why was I feeling like I was banging my head against a wall? The process seemed so simple to me…develop a plan, follow it consistently, and remain accountable to attain whatever goal the team set out to accomplish. That process was effective thus far.

God had another plan, and honestly, going through the resistance was very uncomfortable for me. I felt helpless. The usual methods I had been using for years were getting good results. God decided I needed to learn leadership through the back door, which turned out to be God's first major step of putting me through the fire to talk less and pray more.

I worked with business owners and top executives of fortune 500 companies. I assumed they understood how to manage people, but were not making the same investment in their personal lives or their families. I'm asking, "What's up with that Lord? Where are their priorities?" He decided now I was ready for the answer, and the learning pushed my every button.

I had to go into New York City and meet with an agent and decided to stop by and meet with some other colleagues since I rarely saw them in person. I walked away from a meeting so angry and frustrated, as I went to meet a lady with whom I had done business with over the phone for a couple of years. She told me the owner of the company would like to meet with me. I was open and willing, and as I sat to discuss how we could best collaborate, he started asking me questions I didn't believe were pertinent to do business together. I calmly refused to answer. He only persisted in trying to get an answer from me, and when I refused to answer the third time, he admitted he was manipulating me. He purposefully pressed my buttons to see how I responded when put in an uncomfortable situation. Everything in me was raging. How dare someone be so deceptive and manipulative! However, I remained calm during the entire meeting and decided I would never do business with the company again.

I started ranting to God as I'm riding the train back to Greenwich. When I paused long enough to hear God, these questions came to mind. He asked me, "You know the frustration you've been feeling on the job that people aren't putting the energy you feel necessary to get the results in their personal lives?"

I nodded silently that I heard him. God said, "Imagine what kind of energy you would have when you got home at night after working ten hour days in an atmosphere you just experienced in that meeting?" I hung my head as I sat on the train thinking: Oh no Lord, I don't ever want to work in an atmosphere like that. I imagined the stress I would experience working every day with such a spirit of deception, as I had in that meeting. I would be worn out. I would want to come home and collapse on the couch and rest, knowing I would be going back to the same thing tomorrow. God asked me, "You think maybe now you could give the people you work with a little more grace and mercy as you consider your expectations?"

I immediately went into repentance saying, "Oh yes, Lord, I am so sorry my pride and arrogance got in the way. Help me please?" The Lord then walked me through an intense season of lessons to show grace and mercy to others. I must admit it was one of the toughest seasons I've experienced. When a person emotionally slapped me in the face, I turned the other cheek (Luke 6:29). I knew the person wasn't intentionally trying to hurt me, but attacked me because of the stress level and wounds that needed healing. I could easily call someone on the carpet for not doing their job, but God said, "Be still and show grace and mercy."

God showed me how much I took His grace and mercy for granted on a daily basis. Through these lessons, my heart softened and my mercy grew deeper for others. He wasn't asking me to give anything I hadn't already received from Him. During this season, everywhere I went, it seemed something happened that tested how sensitive I was to the Holy Spirit to show others grace and mercy. People stole money from me, a parent rejected her child outright and a friend abandoned a business agreement. The lack of integrity I witnessed made me cringe on the inside, and yet God kept saying, "Grace and mercy, Lesa, grace and mercy." Through this journey, my intimacy with the Lord grew deeper. I understood more that He is my source for everything.

When God hinted at the principle I was to learn, the process of learning and putting it into practice was truly a whole other level of transformation. God transformed my mind, as I climbed this mountain of grace and mercy and now he was ready to give me the next revelation as I walked this road holding the hand of Jesus.

♥

I sat in a church service during praise and worship, and I was battling this question as to why I encountered these roadblocks for months now. I had heard all the praise and accolades for a job well done, but I didn't see the progress I felt needed to be accomplished. This was a sincere question for the Lord. I wasn't trying to be self-centered, but truly seeking understanding. I stood their worshipping, and He gave me the scenario of Jesus being the humble servant washing the disciples' feet. Jesus was a man of small means and stature by the world's standards. He didn't need a title or prestige, yet people flocked to him, and He was the leader. Jesus taught with gentleness, grace, and love, always giving to people the free will to follow or not. His consistent flow of love never changed despite their choices.

I understood God showed me the gentleness in the leadership of Jesus. It wasn't aggressive. It was bold, but not aggressive. I got the clear picture of the humility in Jesus' leadership, and then God asked me the question, "Didn't you tell me you wanted to be more like My Son?

I shuddered at the thought of what that meant. I said, "Yes, Lord, I did say that, but this was far from what I had in mind. This scenario You have given is like asking Peter to be like your beloved disciple John. Peter had a fiery personality, ready to fight for truth and be the head of your church. John, on the other hand, was completely content being in your presence and spending time with you in worship. Seriously Lord, you want me to put aside all the gifts you've developed in me as a leader and learn to be subtle and go in through the back door to reach the people you're calling?"

"Yes," God said, "that's what I want."

"Lord, how do I even do that?" I asked.

In the days that followed, I spent much time in prayer. He showed me that He had prepared me through recent studies and trainings. I had to let go in the midst of the conflicts happening at work and allow people to fall down hard enough to decide they were ready to make a change.

How easily I could have resolved the issues. Yet, the change wouldn't last in the long run. Everybody involved had to be equally dedicated to the change, which most people don't like. Usually, extreme circumstances happen in a person's life before one decides to get out of their comfort zone and take the necessary action steps to bring the needed change. Maybe a marriage is on the brink of divorce, or a slight heart attack changes one's eating habits, or a child involved with gangs makes a parent wake up and realize the need for intervention.

The wake-up call usually hits hard as one tends to wallow in comfort. I'm just as guilty as the next person of staying in my comfort zone. When God showed me the importance of subtle leadership, I stepped back from situations and asked hard questions of the persons involved. My questions encouraged that they think through the creation of decisive steps to make the desired changes. I watched others fall down in order to arrive at the place God intended to gain the necessary wisdom.

I had to move at God's pace, not at my pace. In order to do this, I learned the process of surrendering everything to God. This was the second mountain He was about to have me climb, as His called me to talk less and pray more.

♥ Reflections

Does God have you on a detour right now? Explain? *He has me on hold.*

Will you share how critical the detour was in order for you to walk in His will today? Others can learn from you. *I hope so*

What lessons have you learned about God's grace and mercy? *It is never ending*

How well do you show grace and mercy to others?

"When you commune with Me in the garden of your heart, both you and I are blessed. This is My way of living in the world – through you! Together we will push back the darkness, for I am the Light of the world."[vi]

Chapter 5

Surrender, Just Pray!

I hold in the forefront of my mind that I'm a vessel for the Lord.

The Lord Jesus showed me clearly that He's holding my hand. He has also shown me time and again that He hears my prayers. Whether it's the encouragement I needed while mourning my brother's death or as I sat at my mother's bedside in the hospital, His presence and glory were tangible. He took me to quiet places with Him, as I walked in a spirit of grace and mercy toward others. He showed me that the results I sought would come through prayer rather than my usual style of teaching and coaching.

For the longest time I told my dedicated intercessors that the two things I needed most from God was clarity and discernment. I always try to hold in the forefront of my mind that I'm a vessel for the Lord whether I'm sitting on a plane, walking into a store, or hanging out with loved ones on the front porch. You might find it hilarious to know that I wouldn't specifically pray for God to give me wisdom.

I learned from studying God's word and from great mentors that there's a price to pay for it. Honestly…I didn't want to go through the battles I had seen many go through to gain wisdom. I would say, "No, no, no Lord I don't want to experience that stuff. I'd rather learn through other people's experiences thank you very much."

Of course, I knew I needed God's guidance constantly as I sought to do His work and be His instrument; so I went through a side door in my prayers and asked for clarity and discernment. I can picture you chuckling and my loving Father up there looking down on me saying, "Okay Lesa, I can let you somehow think that giving you clarity and discernment is going to be an easier road than giving you wisdom, but they are the same thing."

Like God doesn't already know what's going through my mind and what I am trying to run from!

Over the years God has brought into my life some precious ladies, who have a strong gift of mercy (Rom 12:6-8). Honestly, I've openly expressed to others and the Lord I don't want it.

I love and care about people deeply, but God has given a special anointing to people who have the gift of mercy to truly feel people's pain and suffering. My logic wonders why would I want to experience that? I didn't want it, and I've been stubborn with God to resist it. I understand the significance of the gift. The call is to intercede in prayer for others. I believe there would be no better person to go to battle in prayer for me than one who has the gift of mercy.

A person fights the battle differently when experiencing the pain. It's not nonchalant and easy-going to take the sword of truth to defeat the enemy working in a person's life. I'll bet you can guess from the title of this book that a time arrived when I had to surrender and accept this gift from God, if I continued to walk in His will. I've only been given this gift in my present season.

A few years back I got an emergency call from a colleague needing someone to work with a family who had just suffered a tragic accident involving an all-terrain-vehicle. The mom was in the hospital paralyzed from the ribs to her toes. She was driving and lost her seven-year-old son in the accident. Three other children were at home with a young mother's helper to watch over them. Dad needed someone to come and keep stability in the home.

No words truly express the pain a family experiences during a loss. The person feels such grief that they are in the black hole mourning and suffering. People with a gift of mercy can do wonderful ministry during a time like this by standing with them in the darkness; doing their best to comfort them; weeping with them as they feel their pain and cry out to God to heal their broken hearts. The family needed this kind of ministry.

My tendency as the natural exhorter is to pull people out of the dark hole of sadness and suffering, but sometimes, it is totally acceptable to experience pain and sadness due to such events. My first thought was that I wasn't going down in to the darkness. I'd rather wait and pull one out of that dark hole at the right time. However, God had another plan for me that caused me to eventually surrender to His will.

♥

Only in the past few months have I've gained deeper understanding as to my motive behind my prayer for clarity and discernment and why it wasn't Godly. Yet, in His amazing grace and mercy, He still gave me what I requested. I could sit and listen to people, and while doing my best to encourage them, God showed me the depth of the root issues causing the inner battles people fought. I realized my motive was out of selfishness and emotional safety that I prayed for clarity and discernment. I wanted to feel as much in control of situations as humanly possible.

45

Oh, I wasn't thinking that when I prayed for it. I thought in my child-like mind that if I were clear and discerning, I would know how to bring about positive change. I'm not saying to want to make a positive change for God is a bad thing. However, my natural instinct, as a leader to get results as quickly as possible, could get in God's way while He worked in the heart of a person.

God took me through a process that involved a bit of kicking and screaming to truly understand why intercessory prayer is vital. I needed to get out of God's way in order to let Him work in the people around me, as I interceded in prayer. I had to be still and pray when my initial reaction would have been to listen, encourage, and fix the problem.

As I walked down this dirt road with Jesus, I was stumbling on some of the rocks because I let go of His hand. I still walked beside Him, but not hearing Him clearly was the reason I experienced frustration. I was at my wit's end.

I froze. God brought me to the next mountain, and in big, bright lights before me I saw the word SURRENDER. I was turned upside down again. He gave me what I asked for. I had the clarity and discernment and understood the dynamics, but I was getting in God's way. As we started to climb the mountain, I heard God say, "Just because I gave you the clarity and discernment you prayed for doesn't mean I wanted you to do anything about it."

I realized I took the lead before God and needed to repent. I felt so sorrowful for my pride and arrogance, even if my intent was to create positive, loving change. I got down on my knees, raised up my hands, and gave it back to Him. Isn't that what God wants each believer to do…to let go and let Him take the reins? My part was to just PRAY!

I received deeper revelation about God's intimacy with His children. I now understood that prayer was the most significant deed, that is, to pray and to wait, not act to get results, but to pray and to wait. This allowed God to intervene and work in the hearts of the people to bring transformation. People would see more of God and less of me.

God wasn't letting me deal with the surface stuff any longer. He forced me to go deeper and to pray about the root issues occurring in others' souls. The weapon for breakthrough was prayer and is prayer. I couldn't teach it, fix it, or heal it. Most people God had me working with did not have a personal relationship with the Lord or had not received salvation. They had created walls over time to protect their tender hearts from vulnerability and pain.

As recently as last night, I heard pastor Jentezen Franklin during a Wednesday night church service ask, "Are we outwardly empowered or inwardly transformed?" I understood that God wants each person to be inwardly transformed. For that to happen, God draws people to Him and works in their hearts. Only He can do this. I couldn't make that happen, but I could pray more and talk less so the Holy Spirit could work in a person's heart.

As I surrendered to pray more, that God was doing the work became more apparent to those around me. His presence became more real and increased people's faith and belief in Him, as they witnessed the power of God and gave Him the glory. That's ultimately what was supposed to happen anyway, isn't it?

The second mountain He was climbing with me was all about my ability to surrender everything to Him and give God the glory

47

♥ Reflections

Are there instances you can think of right now where God is saying step back from the situation, surrender and let Him do the work as you intercede in prayer?

Can you think of times when you cared so much about another person that you got in the way of God working in their life? Explain?

Do you understand that God loves this person so much more than you can think or imagine?

Have you experienced His freedom by letting go and surrendering everything to God? Describe?

What I search for in My children is an awakened soul that thrills to the Joy of My Presence! I created mankind to glorify me and enjoy Me forever. I provide the Joy; your part is to glorify Me by living close to Me.[vii]

Chapter 6

His Glory or Mine?

God asked, "Is this about you or Me?"

That could be a tough question, couldn't it? When God asked me, the question caused me to stop and ponder. The pause was not short. Rather, I completely stopped what I was doing to consider this. I knew in my heart I wanted to bring glory to the Lord in all that I did. I wanted people to see Jesus every time they interacted with me. Each person fights a daily battle between giving into fleshly desires or submitting to the Holy Spirit to stay on track and walk in the will of God. The more time I spent in prayer and listening to His voice, the easier it became to walk in obedience.

Sometimes I didn't even know I sought the glory or recognition in a situation until the Lord pulled me back, told me to stop what I was doing and pray.

For example, perhaps your child was unhappy about a conversation with his coach after a big game. Your natural instinct was to protect your child and you came to his defense. Many parents would talk to the coach to try and solve the problem. That could help if you had a good relationship with the coach. Yet, the relationship to be restored would be between the child and his coach. The two people involved in the conflict should talk with one another. As a parent, you encourage your son to meet with his coach. You help him be more effective in developing relationships and problem solving. Such instances help him build character. Your son would learn how to deal with conflict effectively. Unfortunately, at times, even when there's disappointment, experience could be our best teacher.

Experiencing love and respect, joy and trials, forgiveness and pain, praise and happiness builds intimacy. The more two people have experienced this together, the deeper their intimacy. Their involvement made intimacy happen based on their investment in the relationship. The parent couldn't create a deeper relationship between the child and the coach. Only the child and coach could do that. The same principle applies to people and their relationship with God.

When I understood this concept, I realized I was in God's way for people to truly see Him. People saw more of me than of God. I surrendered and moved out of the way and dedicated more time to prayer. It wasn't about me. In order for God to receive the glory, any situation had to be very apparent that He was doing the work. The more real God became to a person, the more glory God received.

♥ Reflections

I am sure you can think of instances where you were crying out to God, finally realizing you had to get out of the way and surrender the situation to Him. Maybe you desired so much for your husband to hunger and thirst for a deeper relationship with God? Perhaps your daughter experienced the insecurity of those teen years with all the peer pressure around her? Maybe you felt like the bonds to your brother or sister, whom you love and respect dearly, weren't as tight, and you've experienced a devastating sense of loss? Was it co-workers who had a very condemning nature? Perhaps you felt like darts penetrated through you whenever you were around them?

Prayer is your greatest tool for your breakthrough, whether it's in your marriage, family, church or career. Prayer is the answer! I couldn't change the heart of a person; only God could do that. To see a long-lasting transformation in people's lives a God connection is needed. Often as I'm teaching, I see people nodding yes, confirming they agree with what I'm saying, but change doesn't necessarily happen.

You see it all the time don't you? You go to a church service, attend a conference or spend some time with a fellowship group and you say, "Wow, that teaching was awesome. It was so deep and profound. Let's come up with a plan on how to implement it?" Then you go home, get caught up in the same routine, and stay comfortable even though you were hyped up about the teaching you heard just a few days ago. True change manifests when it comes from deep within. It takes God to knit in your heart that strong desire to change and develop the necessary discipline to bring it to fruition. I understood more clearly now my call to pray in order for God to bring the transformation He desires and receive the glory.

Are there situations in your life where people are seeing more of you and less of God?

Are there instances right now where you are being called to step back and just pray so God can intervene in a person's life or situation?

Are you willing to let go and commit time to pray for those people so God's glory becomes evident?

Will you commit to developing a habit of consistent prayer time with the Lord?

"Father, in the name of Jesus, I am your building under construction—a house of prayer. I abide in You and Your Word abides in me. With the Holy Spirit as my Helper, and by the grace of God, I commit to a life of prayer; I will not turn coward or give up. I desire to become more deeply and intimately acquainted with You, my Father, my Lord and my Savior Jesus Christ. Amen." [viii]

~Brenda Curtiss

Chapter 7

I Teach! How Do I Talk Less and Teach?

My question to the Lord was, "How do I talk less and teach?" Teaching was a big part of my profession as a coach. I have taught, mentored, and encouraged for many years. Truly, God pruned the fruit of self-control in me, and in many ways, it would have been easier for God to tape my mouth so I couldn't speak.

Yet, my loving God, who gave me free will, chose not to be so harsh. He let me learn to do so with self-discipline through my own will. For me to develop this habit, I imagined being tied to my office chair with tape over my mouth, and the only time I could talk was if I chose to pray. Believe me when I tell you it didn't happen overnight.

The Holy Spirit convicted me at times when I said something to someone, who did not receive the message with the love I intended. His correction and reminder was that if I prayed, the situation would work itself out. The Lord had to do the work in the person, and my saying something got in the way. What made the process more difficult was that many times these same individuals sought me for ministry. God told me no, and to just pray.

I spent more time in prayer and I received the clarity that my time to speak was when someone asked me specific questions. This has always been great advice because people really don't want your opinion unless they ask for it. You know the saying that we've been given two ears and one mouth for a reason? The Lord had allowed me to minister to people frequently over the years, and what had become a natural habit for me needed to change for this new season.

♥ Reflections

Can you remember a season in your life when everything that seemed to work before was no longer working? All of this nudging was what I felt while in New York City, and I sensed things were changing in the atmosphere. As I sought Him more, God brought me understanding that much of the work I had done was only touching the surface of people's problems. I took actions steps to fix the problem, but I wasn't getting to the root issues to bring the deeper healing and transformation. The world we live in makes everything look good on the outside, but inside people carry so much pain and rejection.

God showed me His desire was to deal with the root issues, which is not an easy process. It's painful and forces vulnerability. Most people tend to run from it if given the choice. The Holy Spirit showed me the invisible walls people put around themselves for protection. With each person, I tried to be transparent and compassionate, and mostly I received reactive, defensive behavior, as I attempted to open lines of communication. Their behavior showed me they weren't ready.

Moreover, God showed me the wounds and pain people tried to hide, and I realized only God could do the work. The root issues had to be brought to the surface to allow healing. God was the only one who could do this, and my only alternative was to pray. Here I was doing everything in my power until I was at my wits end, getting no results, and all I could do was pray. Isn't that what happens so often in our walk with God?

At this point God didn't care about me teaching as this wouldn't solve the problem or bring the deep healing and transformation so desperately needed. As I prayed, the Lord gave me more compassion. With more compassion I walked in more grace and mercy. He was developing a tenderness within me that allowed me to walk differently in His love.

♥ Reflections

Are there instances in your own life that praying would be more effective than confronting issues so God can work in the situation?

Have you experienced peace in the midst of the storm because you prayed and surrendered it to the Lord? Describe?

What wisdom would you share with other believers regarding the power of prayer?

Has the discipline of praying more and talking less been easy or difficult for you to learn? Why?

Overcoming Satan

"As a Christian I must seek to overcome not only the world but also satan. He is a more deadly foe than the world, because the world is simply a pawn in his hand (1 John 5:19).

"The world will tantalize and tease me, but satan will accuse me (Rev 12:10).

"And call upon Me in the day of trouble; I shall rescue you, and you will honor Me" (Ps. 50:15) [ix]

Chapter 8

Surrender Again!

A Warrior's Call to Intercession

I stepped out of the way to pray more for God's glory, and people thought something was wrong, as I seemed withdrawn to them and not as social during gatherings. I put myself through this daily discipline to develop the self-control to only listen to conversations and pray by the leading of the Holy Spirit. It was tough! I practiced severe amounts of self-control to not give the answer to help when God, not me, was the one who would heal. I was sure many husbands and wives, understand and experience this very thing when building a strong relationship with each other. If that were not the case, there wouldn't be so many best-selling books out there such as *The Power of a Praying Wife.* This season took me much deeper in my relationship with God and the call to be His intercessor. This is the third mountain He climbed with me, the mountain of intercession.

Have you ever walked into certain places like homes, businesses, or churches and sensed something wasn't quite right? You can't necessarily pinpoint what it is, but some type of warning goes off inside of you. As God gave me His discernment, this happened to me more and more. I would be visiting a home, sitting by myself in front of my laptop, and suddenly strong feelings of anxiety would come over me out of nowhere. I looked to God, thinking what's up with this? I am not a person who has ever experienced anxiety. It took me a while to analyze these feelings, and I'd start to pray and later realize something was going on in the atmosphere. I would need to fight the battle with the sword of the spirit by praying, as Paul states in Ephesians 6:17-19.

As I prayed, the anxious feelings would go away for a while. This occurred two to three times a week, and each time I prayed in the spirit, the feelings diminished. Not only was I praying for God's will to be done, but also in my own selfishness, I was telling God that He could take these feelings and just do away with them altogether. I did not like all these emotions rising up inside of me, feeling out of control for no apparent reason. This was not my nature at all.

That's our wish isn't it? To be in control of everything in our lives, and when we can't be in control, we fight it out with others and with God. Vulnerability causes fear to rise in people. There is fear of rejection, pain, failure, shame, and vulnerability itself. Yet, the more authentic and real a person becomes, the deeper the intimacy and emotional fulfillment he or she will experience in his life.

As I experienced all of these feelings that I did not understand, I started thinking about all the brothers and sisters in Christ who have the gift of compassion and mercy that Paul talks about in Romans 12:8.

I'm thinking oh no, Lord, that's what this feels like? I do not want this Lord! I was like a child kicking and screaming in rebellion, not wanting to serve God in this way. I understood He had taped my mouth and told me to pray more, but this? This was different and God knew I would never ask for this spirit of mercy.

A month went by and I decided to bring in the New Year by attending a conference. I felt the need to soak in God's presence for three days, seek Him and gain understanding. The conference offered certain times to receive a word of prophecy. I bet you can guess what happened?

When a prophetic word is given, it's usually confirmation of something God has already began working in the person. Or at least, that's been my journey with the Lord thus far. The second day at the conference I chatted with a group, as we hung out between sessions. A gentleman walked up to me, and as he's passing by with a smile on his face, he said, "You got a word for me?" I smiled and told him, "No, I don't." However, he had a word for me. I froze thinking, here it comes.

He said, "You are a strong warrior for the Lord. You are being called to stand on top of the watchtower and intercede for His church. Your strong faith and dedication to Him needs you fighting the battles in the spirit realm about the bigger things occurring in the world."

I didn't respond. My facial expression showed I wasn't receiving this joyfully. I knew the responsibility that came with this assignment. The man understood my facial expression and continued on his way. The people standing next to me were excited. I told them I wasn't and explained why.

The man returned a few seconds later and said, "Oh and I forgot to tell you, the Lord is going to send people to stand beside you during this process. You won't be doing it alone." My response was muted...well that's good...but I was still being stubborn.

As prophetic ministry was offered at the conference, I debated on whether to attend. I stood fighting the mental battle, as I didn't want to surrender to what God told me. Finally, I just walked back into the sanctuary. I wept before the Lord. I knew if I went any further to deny what He was telling me, I would be in complete rebellion. There was no question based on my recent experiences with God that He had given me direction. I was now at the point of repentance. I sat there in my seat admitting my selfishness, wanting to serve Him my way...the comfortable way!

I eventually surrendered to His will once again. As I sat there duking it out internally to surrender, I knew why I was fighting it so hard. I didn't want to deal with all these feelings of mercy and pain I see intercessors experience. I felt I am sensitive enough as it is. I didn't need to become more sensitive was my fear-based logical thinking, and the Lord knew it long before I did.

Once I got to the point of surrender, the Lord showed me the simplicity of how not to carry the fear. When given this gift of mercy to intercede for others and feel other people's pain and struggle, the assignment, as a prayer warrior, is to take it before God, stand on the promises of His Word and take full authority over the enemy.

A warrior is not supposed to hold the burdens of those feelings, but release them to the Lord instead. I didn't have to carry the emotions. All I had to do was go before the Lord on behalf of His people and release everything to Him in prayer. Because God gave us free will, we need to go to Him in prayer. He can't help us if we don't ask. I think you'll agree that a person prays very differently when connected by strong emotions to the people and situations they are praying about. It may be a marriage that's about to fall apart, a child who needs a miracle to live after a bad car crash, or a family member dying of cancer. Those emotions are strong and raw and causes one to be the most vulnerable, as they cry out to God. The prayers aren't lackadaisical; they are fierce and strong in His might and power. I always considered myself truly blessed, as fellow brothers and sisters in Christ with a strong gift of mercy, consistently interceded for me. I knew they were standing in the gap, fighting battles the enemy had brought upon me through prayer by the power of the Holy Spirit. Who better to stand beside me than those who experienced my feelings and prayed against any obstacles the enemy tried to use to make me stumble. Now my turn had arrived for me to do the same.

I accepted the assignment. I would commit time to intercede for the kingdom of God, and I would start with an hour a day.

♥

If I consider the dream as I walked down the dirt road with Jesus, this was a time when I tried to pull Him in the direction I wanted to walk on my terms, like I wanted to turn back and walk along the road of familiarity. Doing so made me feel safe because I knew the terrain, what was already there. My heart wanted to follow Him, but not pay the price to move forward into the calling God had for me. I was holding His hand but trying to pull Him back to a place of comfort.

Instead I was standing still and I couldn't move forward until I surrendered and obeyed the call. As the Lord climbed this mountain of intercession with me, the burden became lighter, and I changed. He renewed my hope, and I depended on Him more and more.

♥ Reflections

Can you recall a time when God called you to a certain assignment and you fought Him kicking and screaming not wanting to obey?

How did the Lord get you to surrender to the call?

What wisdom would you share with others, who might be experiencing this?

"We come to Christ and a new day begins. Yet the Lord's day begins at evening, not morning (Gen. 1:5). It is here, as evening turns to night, that God teaches us to walk by faith. It is in this place—where we can hear but cannot see—that we learn to trust the word God whispers to us in the darkness (Matt. 10:27).

"Dawn will come, beloved. When it does you will see that it was during the night that God made you a true person of faith. The word He whispered to you—the living word that saved, you held it fast—you will proclaim in the light. And what changed you, will change others also." [x]

~Francis Frangipane, In Christ's Image Training

Chapter 9

Accepting the Call

As I walked in obedience and committed time in prayer, I asked the Lord to give me specific things to pray about. I wrote a list when ideas came to mind as I sat there quietly. God put on my heart concepts that were big battles, such as abortion, human trafficking, divorce, political leaders, people serving in our military, as well as healing and wholeness for His church. When you consider the assignment of an intercessor, the anointing of high authority is given to this person in God's army. The anointing is a call to defeat the enemy regarding kingdom principles. By the power of the Holy Spirit the prayer warrior receives clarity on the works of the enemy. God provides discernment so the battle can be won.

The Interceding Disciple

"I can never become one of God's intercessors without remembering that Jesus Christ" made intercession for the transgressors" (Isaiah 53:12). That statement means more than the fact that Jesus prayed for His crucifers or makes atonement for us. It means He created the office or function of intercession. He made intercession possible. Had He not come as the great interceding Savior, no one could ever have interceded for anyone else.

"For me to become an intercessor, then, means that I am fulfilling a function that Jesus Christ created, that I am doing it for His sake and in His wake. It also means that I have gained a certain level in my

65

relationship to God in which I have gained a certain authority in intercession. Norman P. Grubb calls this "the grace of faith." That is not a single answer to prayer, but a whole series of answers based upon my definite standing with God as an intercessor. For example, Moses reached an intimacy with God that he talked with God "face to face" (Exodus 33:11). As a result of this extremely high privilege, Moses was able to use his authority as an intercessor to save Israel from certain extinction because of their sin in the matter of the golden calf (Exodus 32:10). Had Moses not been there, in the high, holy position of Israel's intercessor, the nation would have been obliterated.

"I think of others who have been there, and I have been challenged! What about Isaiah, Jeremiah, Ezekiel, Hosea, Paul, Luther, Wesley, and countless others for whose sake people were given the gift of life? Lord, I want to be an interceding disciple, capable of sparing from death and bringing to life those for whom Jesus Christ died! I cannot appoint myself to this ministry (even Jesus did not do that, Hebrews 5:5), but I can live devoted to Him so that He may not pass me by when next He needs an intercessor." xi

My heart sincerely wanted to be obedient to my Father in heaven. After a couple of weeks, I found it difficult to sit for an hour and pray. As a Type A personality, I naturally focused on time and thought of it being completed after an hour. I had to change my thinking about that. Instead of trying to figure out what I should be praying about, I continued to pray in tongues through the Holy Spirit. I figured the Holy Spirit knew far more than I did about what God wanted from His intercessors. Some moments God would put something specific on my heart to pray for, and I followed through. I was still determined to dedicate an hour in prayer and meditation to the Lord. I even used a timer set for one hour so I would stay focused. This was about disciplining myself to create a habit, like a runner who is dedicated to health and commits to running daily.

Although I understood the gift of praying in tongues, I must confess until now I did very little of this type of praying. This was a God-given assignment, and I was going to fulfill the call. God brought me deeper revelation, as I read devotionals and studied His Word. I interacted with others, and I saw more vulnerability. I felt God's spirit of compassion and mercy upon me. I knew why. It was my call to pray. As easy as it would have been for me to minister and encourage, the Lord said, "No, I just want you to pray." He showed me that as I prayed, His Holy Spirit would work in the hearts of the people, and they would see more of God and draw closer to Him. That's our ultimate goal, right? He wants that close intimacy with each of us.

He wants to be the first one you call upon no matter the circumstances in your life. He wants to hear your praises and gratitude when something great happens, and He wants to hear your heart's cry when there's pain and disappointment. God wants to be an every-moment-God in your life.

The more I listened and asked questions for a person to ponder and to seek God and His word, the more healing I witnessed. This was followed by more glory God received. I understood it isn't always that simple. Sometimes when people are seeking advice or counsel, they aren't ready to go through the necessary steps to receive the healing. They want God to be the magic genie in a bottle and make everything instantly better.

I am sure almost every person can recall a time when they perceived God as the magician with the name it, claim it, and receive it type of prayer. By studying His word, one realizes God's motive is to love us and mold us to be more like Christ, not instantly to fix us.

As I remained persistent praying daily before the Lord, He put on my heart, the restoration of marriages and families...to bring healing and wholeness to those relationships and intentionally make God the center of their lives. If healing could be brought to families, then the rest of the destruction happening in the world would go away... the abuse, adultery, divorce, human trafficking, gang affiliation, murder, drug addiction, lack of integrity in our government leaders due to a drive for power and greed that is followed by deceit and manipulation.

I prayed daily for months, and suddenly issues like the pain of sexual abuse or rape that people had carried for years surfaced. My prayers were answered as God brought the root issues of wounds to the surface so His children could be set free from the bondage. Satan had them for so long and now God's healing power was piercing through the strongholds of the enemy! The spirit of mercy became stronger in me as people shared their stories. There were moments I felt helpless and tears would come to my eyes as I listened. I wanted to make it all better, but I could only show them love and pray.

During this time I worked with a client who carried some large, open, emotional wounds that were deep and painful. Almost every response from her was instantly defensive. It felt as if she had sharp claws that swiped across my cheek at every interaction. Her words were critical and condemning. By the revelation of the Holy Spirit, I realized the root cause of her actions were fear and rejection. I ached for her and the destructive affect her actions were having on her marriage and her children. By God's grace, He gave me the ability to speak with her calmly. In this manner, I spoke truth into her life, and she didn't know how to respond. She was accustomed to fighting back and defending herself. She couldn't emotionally handle being wrong for fear of failure. As tough and strong as she seemed on the outside, she was hurting, desperate for acceptance, and crumbling on the inside while running in a spirit of perfectionism. She was an adult bully. God told me to just pray. As much as I wanted to help her, I knew only God could do the necessary work.

I wept night after night in prayer. At one point I even got mad at God, asking why He just wouldn't fix it? He's all-powerful! He's capable of performing these miracles. What's up! Why am I fighting this battle day after day and going through all these emotions. Then he reminded me of the revelation he gave me just a few months before when He woke me up at 4 a.m. that I share with you in the next chapter.

♥ Reflections

What has God put on your heart to pray about for His kingdom?

Are there specific issues that stir a passion inside of you? Maybe unwed mothers, abortion, or those fighting cancer? Write them down as they come to mind as you seek the Lord. *trafficking   world peace*

Have you considered that God has given you a certain passion or sensitivity because He's called you to pray?

Would you be willing to commit yourself to praying for those areas, as a service to God and His kingdom?

God's Tear Bottle

"I am comforted when I realize that God is not a vast computer, but a feeling, emotional person, a grander image of myself. He loves, hates, pities, and sympathizes.

"Nothing proves His large heart of sympathy more than David's words, 'Put my tears in Thy bottle; are they not in Thy book?' (Psalm 56:8). God has a personal tear bottle for every one of His children; therefore, there is no sorrow He does not notice and no tear He does not record. Sometimes I weep in public and sometimes in private, but private or public, God catches my fallen tears and saves them...

"How full is my personal tear bottle, now resting in the Lord's hands? It may never be as full as that of Jeremiah, who wondered 'if any sorrow (was) like unto his sorrow' (Lamentations 1:12, KJV); or like that of Paul, who 'glorified' in his sufferings for Christ's sake (2 Corinthians 11:8,23); and certainly not like that of Christ, whose tear bottle was big enough to hold the tears of the whole world. Do I weep over my own sins as Job did? Have I broken my heart over the hardness of men as Ezekiel did?

"One day God will give me back my tear bottle – whether full or only partly so – and then I will have the privilege of doing what the woman did: pouring it over the feet of Him who both collects and rewards my tears (Luke 7:36-38). Then He will wipe away all tears from my eyes forever (Revelation 21:4).

'The Lord your God is in your midst, a victorious warrior. He will exult over you with joy, He will be quiet in His love, He will rejoice over you with shouts of joy'"[xii] (Zephaniah 3:17)

70

Chapter 10

Aching for Those You Love

I avoided writing this chapter because it was the toughest.

Ask yourself this penetrating question: What if the very reason God allows conflict or pain with a person in your life is because you are the person God has equipped to pray for them?

The call to intercede requires a person to go boldly before God in prayer to fight battles He's assigned to the intercessor. There are also individual battles you may be facing in your daily life. As the Lord moved me into this season of praying more and talking less, I received clarity about the people around me, both on the job and in my personal life. We all have them don't we?

Would we run from the people in our lives, if given the choice, because of pain or frustration we experience? You stand in the same room with a certain person and feel all kinds of negative emotions rise inside of you. As Christians we know it is God's utmost command to love one another. Yet, when the pain happens between you and a person for whom you care deeply, like a parent, a spouse, a child, a mentor, or a pastor, you feel like the pain is multiplied.

You cry out to the Father in heaven praying for healing and restoration. You don't want to hurt any more. Yet, what if the Lord allows this to happen because you are the only person in their life equipped to pray for them, or they may not be saved and know the Lord, Jesus Christ. There may be battles and serious bondage they are living with, and they are unaware because the enemy has blinded their spiritual eyes. They are clueless as to how to be set free. Your prayers could determine their salvation and freedom in Christ.

Honestly, I avoided writing this chapter because this is the toughest chapter of the book. However, as God showed me how He had put all the pieces of the puzzle together to get me to the point of surrender and spend time interceding in prayer, I knew I would write this book. I opened up my laptop, started putting chapters in order and began to write. I wrote the first draft of the previous chapters in two weeks, and then I procrastinated for days. I started to write again, but didn't know where to start. I actually put the manuscript aside for a year.

I had a pain that was still so raw in me that I cried out to the Lord. The pain stemmed from years of rejection and abandonment by an influential adult figure I had once respected. There were days I wanted to just walk away and not feel the pain...to block it out. I knew I couldn't do this because the only way to get the breakthrough would be to bring the issue to the surface so God could bring the healing.

It seemed like forever that I had cried out to God. I chose to walk in forgiveness and tried to connect with this person showing them love and encouragement. It's inevitable that we crossed paths because of common social circles. I tried to keep the lines of communication open, and each time I did so, I saw the person shut down, unwilling to talk about the issues that caused the division in the relationship. Eventually the person would not acknowledge my presence when I walked into a room with a small group of people. The pain felt like a sword stabbing through my heart and pulled out again, leaving me to bleed.

The Lord showed me the insecurities and wounds this person carried. I finally understood the behaviors had nothing to do with me. The behaviors were due to the person's longer-term wounds that hadn't healed. The spirit of fear, rejection, and abandonment that haunted this person could no longer be covered up with a spirit of high achievement to feel accepted and worthy. The spiritual warfare was so strong in the atmosphere as the presence of the Holy Spirit penetrated the darkness to bring the truth to light. (Luke 11:33-35NASB)This person wasn't ready to be vulnerable and instead remained silent.

Finally, I got to a point in the silent battle with this person where I turned my anger to God. I believed I was doing all the right things to bring healing to the relationship, yet still the pain and division remained. It wasn't fair! I didn't deserve the rejection and abandonment when I had been walking in love and obedience. This person had once shown me love and nurtured me, and now all I felt was rejection, abandonment, and judgment.

"God," I cried, "Tell me why?"

Desperately, helplessly, longingly, I cried:
Quietly, patiently, lovingly God replied.
I pled and I wept for a clue to my fate...
And the Master so gently said, "Wait."

WAIT? You say, "Wait?" my indignant reply.
Lord, I need answers. I need to know why!
Is your hand shortened? Or have you not heard?
By Faith I have asked and am claiming your Word.

My future and all to which I relate
Hangs in the balance and YOU tell me "Wait?"
I'm needing a 'yes', a go-ahead sign,
Or even a 'no' to which I can resign.

You promised, dear Lord, that if we believe,
We need but to ask, and we will receive.
And, Lord I've been asking, and this is my cry:
I'm weary of asking! I need a reply!"

Then quietly, softly, I learned of my fate
As my Master replied once again, "Wait."
So I slumped in my chair, defeated and taut.
And grumbled to God, "So, I'm waiting for what?"

He seemed then, to kneel, and His eyes met with mine,
And He tenderly said, "I could give you a sign.
I could shake the heavens and darken the sun.
I could raise the dead, cause the mountains to run.

I could give all you seek and pleased you would be.
You would have what you want, but you wouldn't
know Me.
You'd not know the depth of My love for each saint.
You'd not know the power that I give to the faint.

You'd not learn to see through clouds of despair;
You'd not learn to trust just by knowing I'm there;
You'd not know joy of resting in me
When darkness and silence were all you could see.

You'd never experience that fullness of love,
When the peace of My Spirit descends like a dove.
You would know that I give, and I save, for a start,
But you'd not know the depth of the beat of My Heart.

The glow of My comfort late into the night,
The faith that I give when you walk without sight.
The depth that's beyond getting just what you ask
From an infinite God, who makes what you have last.

You'd never know, should your pain quickly flee,
What it means that, "My grace is sufficient for thee."

Yes, your dearest dreams overnight would come true,
But, oh, the loss, if you missed what I'm doing in you.

So be silent, My child, and in time you will see
That the greatest of gifts is to truly know Me.
And though oft may My answers seem terribly late,
My most precious answer of all is still, "WAIT"[xiii].

♥

Several years passed before I was ready to wash my hands of the relationship. I experienced outright rejection from this person, who refused to call me or include me when important events took place. I had reached my limit of crying out to the Lord to restore the relationship. I was angry, hurt, and wounded. I did all the right things and felt like I was being punished for it.

"That's it, Lord, I'm done." I had forgiven the person for the pain he had caused me and for his lack of knowledge because of their own heavy baggage. The real question was would I allow myself to be subjected to this person's rejection and judgment because the person carried a strong spirit of pride, jealousy, and envy. I did my best to walk in a spirit of grace and mercy while knowing this person wasn't walking in the saving knowledge of Jesus Christ. Finally, I set strong boundaries and decided any connection between me and this person would only happen on the person's initiative.

Of course, as I set this boundary, the Lord would show me a huge revelation...one that brought a breakthrough for others and me.

I traveled during this time doing ministry. Many people needed prayer and encouragement regarding relationship conflicts. God gave me clarity to offer insight and suggestions based on His Word. The Lord woke me up at four o'clock one morning and posed the question that I asked you at the beginning of this chapter. He asked me, "What if the very reason I allow such conflict to happen is because you are the only person in this individual's life who is equipped to pray for their salvation?"

I froze at such a revelation. As I meditated on this, it took my eyes off me and turned them back to the Lord. It now became about God and His kingdom and not about the relationship and my pain. This reinforces a concept mentioned previously…that any person prays differently when emotionally involved.

I felt the pain, the loss, the anger, and disappointment. It was a call from God to pray as a warrior in command to defeat the enemy. I saw the urgency and necessity to pray for a person's soul. God showed me the bigger picture. This relationship hasn't been restored, as I write this, but I remain obedient to love and pray for the person. I don't think this person has a dedicated Christian in his life, who prays for him.

As a believer, I don't want people I care about to go to hell. The enemy will do everything to steal, kill, and destroy, but Jesus came for us to have life and have it more abundantly (Luke 10:10). As I sought the Lord and gained further understanding, I realized He allowed me to go through this to prepare me for intercession. My anger toward God subsided and I prayed more through the Holy Spirit. I experienced His peace and less of the pain.

I'll confess there have been times when I don't feel good toward God about this, but my heart was dedicated long ago to His service, so…I'll wait. For me to think that this journey on earth isn't going to involve pain, rejection, and persecution would be kidding myself when Jesus suffered far more than I will have to in my lifetime.

This 4 a.m. revelation has allowed me to walk in grace and mercy. I wanted to hug this person and have prayed for God to bring healing. God has walked me through humility and grace, as I had opportunities to serve this person, as I was requested. I knew it was difficult to ask me for help, yet I could show her love through acts of service, as Jesus would do, and I was thankful to do this. Seeds were planted as I continued to walk in obedience.

After God spoke to me at 4 a.m., I called the people who had come to me for ministry to share the revelation the Lord gave me. A few months went by and breakthroughs happened in these families. People rededicated their lives to the Lord. Some received healing from terrible child abuse, and others repented for adultery and remained committed to their marriages. All of this was a lesson of surrender and obedience to pray, and in His perfect timing, God moved on behalf of my prayers.

Reflecting on my dream of walking with Jesus, this time the Lord showed me His promise to take me around the rocks in the road if I would trust Him. Even if the rock or obstacle put before me became uncomfortable or scary, when I chose to hold His hand and let Him direct me, everything would be all right. I trusted that victory would prevail.

♥ Reflections

Has someone caused you pain, and you may be the very person to intercede in prayer for their salvation or healing?

What has God revealed to you about this person that allows you to show them grace and mercy?

As you pray to the Father do you experience more of His peace in the midst of the spiritual battle?

Do you see changes happening as God works in the situation because you chose to pray?

A Raging Fire

"Resentment is the cocaine of the emotions. It causes our blood to pump and our energy to rise. But, also like cocaine, it demands increasingly large and more frequent dosages.

There is a dangerous point at which anger ceases to be an emotion and becomes a driving force. A Person bent on revenge moves unknowingly further and further away from being able to forgive, for to be without the anger is to be without a source of energy.

Hatred is the rabid dog that turns on its owner.

Revenge is the raging fire that consumes the arsonist.

Bitterness is the trap that snares the hunter.

And mercy is the choice that can set them all free" [xiv]

Chapter 11

Forgiveness is a Necessity Not an Option

The healing starts with forgiveness.

Are you walking around with a broken heart, carrying open wounds from your past, or need God's healing from the pain of rejection? God wants to heal you completely and bring wholeness to your soul. (3 John 1:2).

He desires to encompass you with His love and peace. I beg of you not to the let a spirit of un-forgiveness take hold of you and carry anger or bitterness.

Jesus said, "Whenever you stand praying, forgive, if you have anything against anyone, so that your Father who is in heaven will also forgive you your transgressions. But if you do not forgive, neither will your Father who is in heaven forgive your transgressions." (Mark 11:25)

Satan has deceived many of God's children with a spirit of confusion about forgiveness. According to the scripture, forgiveness is an action step...to stand before God and say, "I forgive a person for hurting me or violating me in any way." Forgiveness is not based on a feeling or a law of justice that the person deserves to be forgiven. Rather, forgiveness is a simple act of obedience and faith that God will take care of the situation.

I recall a great example being given by a dear sister, Dottie Brock, in one of my fellowship groups. She explained how destructive un-forgiveness could be in a person's life by sharing this analogy. Imagine this...

♥ Reflections

You have a biking accident that causes a one-inch, deep cut in your calf. You could do one of three things. First, you could leave it alone, lose a lot of blood, and allow an infection because you did not clean and bandage the wound. Second, you could stop the bleeding by putting a bandage on the wound, but still risk infection for not cleaning it. Or you could choose the third option, clean the wound, add some antibiotic dressing to help the healing, and cover it with a bandage. If you chose options one or two, you must remember that when the wound gets infected, the infection could spread throughout your entire body.

It's the same way with the poison of un-forgiveness; it affects every area of your life. That wound you carry needs healing and affects not only the relationship with the person who hurt you, but also affects everybody else around you. The spirit of un-forgiveness grows deeper and stronger, and turns from anger to bitterness to resentment to hatred.

You cannot afford to walk in un-forgiveness and live a healthy life. I believe one of the stumbling blocks satan puts in front of God's children is the belief that they haven't forgiven a person when they still experience pain each time they think of the person or an event.

Forgiveness is not based on a feeling. Forgiveness is a decision and an action step. Consider the wound from the bike accident. Let's say that you make the right decision to treat the wound by cleaning it, adding an antibiotic ointment, and covering the wound with a bandage. The wound will heal, but there could still be pain and discomfort during the healing process. To extend the metaphor, your emotional wounds will take time and some discomfort occurs also while God is healing you. When you continue to walk in forgiveness, the pain lessens over time, and eventually the wound is healed. To do this requires a step of faith and belief in God's word regardless of the present pain.

You'll find joy and peace and freedom in Christ Jesus, as you have forgiveness toward others. You receive the love that God wants to pour into your life. Knowingly receiving His love allows you to understand God's ability to bring wholeness if you choose to forgive. He's commanded forgiveness because He knows how the poison of not doing so damages and destroys every relationship in your life. Moreover, un-forgiveness spreads infection and hinders your intimacy with the Father in heaven.

I experienced the healing power of God when I walked away from a relationship three months before my wedding that would have happened over a decade ago. I prayed to know God's will. I knew beyond any doubt that God only wanted what was best for me, yet I needed His clarity to move forward. God showed me the red flags that made it clear…His will was for me not to marry this man. My heart broke at the loss of the relationship, and I dearly loved his family. I didn't want to lose my connection with them regardless of whether this man was a part of my life. I went through the day-to-day healing of this loss, and I was committed to walk in forgiveness. Every time this person came to my mind, I spoke forgiveness about the situation. I believe God quickened the healing of my heart and blessed me beyond what I could imagine in order to maintain a close relationship with his family. They loved and accepted me regardless of the circumstances. In many ways my connection with his family became much more authentic and deeper after I ended the relationship. I don't believe I would have received this blessing had I not chosen to walk in forgiveness. In a very short period, my heart healed and I experienced exhilarating freedom from the bondage the relationship brought to my life. As time went by, I received many confirmations that I had been obedient, as this person has married, divorced and remarried.

I continued to hold the hand of Jesus walking down the dirt road, and God gave me a better understanding about the hindrance of un-forgiveness. He gave me a vision of God being in heaven, looking down on His children. GOD yearned to pour His spirit upon them and send His army of angels to fight against the works of satan. Each time one of His children chose un-forgiveness, His hands were tied by ropes stopping Him from using His healing power. He was waiting patiently for His child's obedience, and as one chose to forgive, the rope was cut and God's hands were freed. His Holy Spirit moved to bring God's comfort and healing. His angels moved to work not only in the individual who forgave, but also in everyone involved in the situation.

I learned how vital is to remember that if you have been wronged or hurt by someone, you are not the change agent in their lives. God is the change agent, the one who transforms from the inside out. You have to depend on Him and not your own knowledge, strength, and power. If you want God to work in your situation, forgiveness is a necessity, not an option as God is our vindicator.

♥ Reflections

Is God bringing someone to mind you need to forgive?

Can you describe the difference in your relationships when you are walking in forgiveness versus un-forgiveness?

Can you share changes you witnessed as God worked in a situation because of your obedience to forgive?

Are there areas you need to trust God more in order to forgive?

The Pain God Feels

"I must avoid at all costs two mistaken ideas of God,
prevalent in our time: that God is above pain, and second,
that God is below manipulation. That God is not above
pain is clear in the Bible; yet the impressions I get from
fellow Christians is that God is as impervious to pain as
He is to sin. Wrong! The two are not synonymous. God
feels pain deeply. He can be "grieved," "wearied,"
"sorrowed," and everything else that represents distress
over disobedience in His children. And what about the
pain of Calvary, the pain not only of the Son but also of
the Father? It was there the blood of God (Acts 20:28) was
shed.

"God suffers pain only in contact with sin. The closer the
person is to God, the sharper will be the pain in the heart
of God over any sin that may appear in him. One of the
"groanings" of Jesus was over the betrayal of Judas, one
of the Twelve (John 13:21). He wounded Jesus far more
deeply that he wounded himself, so I have the capability of
wounding and hurting the One who is the universe to me.
In my trifling with sin, I may not realize how deeply I stab
the heart of Him who bought me at so great a price.

"God is not the distant, sterile judge we often make Him
out to be. If He is that to us, then we have a sadly
inadequate and insufficient view of sin. If I have a
permissive view of sin, then God's pain becomes a mere
trifling irritation that is easily shrugged off. To see what
sin is, I must see Calvary, for there God took its odious,
repulsive measure for all eternity. To see what salvation
from sin is, I must see my living Intercessor who is able to
"sympathize with our weaknesses" and who provides a
throne of grace where my sin burden is dealt with until His
– and my – pain is gone (Hebrews 4:15-16)"[xv]

Chapter 12

Yes Is Better

Have you ever worked with a two-year-old child? I love children at this age. They are so innocent and transparent, as they begin to stand for independence and learn to say "no." This stage can be hilarious and yet frustrating because "no" seems to be the automatic word no matter the request or statement being made. I see this often in my career as I work with parents and families. I do my best to take a positive approach to change the behavior by redirecting, reinforcing the positive, and setting healthy boundaries. Recently I worked with a two-year-old going through her "no" stage, and God decided there would be some significant lessons for me to learn as well. I typically redirect a child by saying, "Yes is better," when they automatically say no and are not cooperating.

The scenario might be that we are going to the park and play. In my enthusiastic voice of telling her we can get ready to go to the park now, but need to clean up the toys before we go, she immediately says, "No." My response is, "Yes is better." She understands that in the relationship I've established with her I am consistent in what I say and do; so we are not going to the park until we complete the cleanup. Eventually, I got to the point where I could pause and not say anything. After a few seconds, she says to me, "Yes is better, Lesa."

I look at her with love and a smile and say, "That is right, yes is better." We clean up and off to the park we go to play.

As I spent time in prayer with the Lord, He brought this message to show to me how often I do this with Him, even in the simplest matter, such as, I attend an event when I'd rather stay home and read a great book. Or it could be more significant, such as a move to Hong Kong for an extensive period of time.

Several months passed before I truly understood the depth of what God was trying to show me. At first I acknowledged that I heard Him and sort of shrugged it off as just being my human nature, like the two-year-old girl. God nudged me to do something, and I squirmed and stayed in my comfort zone. Then He continued nudging until I realized this: If I was going to walk in his will, I must submit to Him and the request He's made of me.

As the Holy Spirit gave me much deeper insight as to how this affects my relationship with God, the message went right to the core of my soul. I cried in sorrow for my disobedience. God brought me back to the importance of being a cheerful giver (2 Cor. 9:7). God doesn't want to be served with grumbling and complaining.

We all do it to some extent even if it's not intentional. I usually keep a similar mindset when giving to and receiving from others. I don't want something from somebody when I sense it is not being done joyfully. I can recall when I've reached out to people for help, and their reaction gives me all kinds of negative feelings. Immediately, I will try and find other options. They might be willing to fulfill my request, but not joyfully; so I bow out gracefully and try not to offend them. It hurts sometimes, as there are some people I would like to count on, and they let me down.

On this particular night when my feelings were hurt, I quietly sat with the Lord pondering this situation. He asked me, "Do you do this with me?" I paused, reflected with immediate scenarios coming to mind, and answered, "Yes I do, Lord." I could picture the scenarios when I've out-rightly refused and stated there were certain things I didn't want to do. A great example is my rebellion in accepting God's gift of mercy, knowing what it entailed, and the responsibility that followed. Another time involved the demands I required God to fulfill if I were to move to Hong Kong. As God let me experience the pain of someone, who I wanted to depend on, letting me down, He asked me, "How do you think this makes Me feel when you say no?"

My heart just broke, and I started sobbing as I imagined how much I had hurt my Father's feelings. I knew through faith that my Father in heaven would never ask me to do anything He hadn't equipped me to do or that wasn't in my best interest. Yet in my selfishness for comfort, I turned away and refused His request. I was overwhelmed with sorrow as I imagined how much this breaks God's heart when He knows what's best for me yesterday, today and forever. He's doing His best to guide me in my daily walk with Him, and in my free will, I refused certain opportunities He put in front of me.

It was a spiritual breakthrough for me to set aside my comforts and renew my commitment to serve Him, regardless of the discomforts or inconveniences in my life. No more whining or complaining, just surrender and truly serve Him as a cheerful giver.

I considered the importance of saying yes to God when I go back to the dream of walking down the dirt road with Jesus. I saw myself letting go of His hand. I was too comfortable and secure with His love and grace that I would go in my own direction according to my wants, needs, and comfort level. He knew that I would eventually return to Him and take His hand. Yet, the pain of letting me walk away, and distance myself from Him, because I wasn't willing to obey the call, must have been heartbreaking for Him.

God's heart so wants the love and closeness of His children that it's not about "the work" I do for Him, as much as the intimacy He desires to have with me. It is the very purpose for which He created man at the beginning of time. Everything He asks me to do is to make me more like Christ and draw me closer to Him. It correlates with the same desire a loving parent has in wanting the best for their child. A parent will love, teach, sacrifice, and give a child free will to help them become the person God has called them to be. It can be painful when being rejected or not listened to, yet it has to be done in order for the growth and development to occur in a child's character. Finally you come to an understanding that "Yes is better." Do trust and know that God always has your best interest no matter the discomfort or obstacle in front of you.

♥ Reflections

Can you recall a time when you have chosen to rebel against God and refused a call or request?

When did the turning point happen for you to surrender and say, "Yes it better?"

As you meditate on this can you see God's profound grace and mercy as He continues to love you through the process?

What area of your life right now might God be nudging you to say, "Yes" to Him?

"Lord, I desire to be a watered garden and to ride on the high places of the earth; but help me to see that I cannot get them by seeking them, but by seeking to feed the afflicted soul and by seeking to do Your will." (Psalm 118:5-6)

Chapter 13

You Have the Victory, Receive it Boldly!

Contemplating the journey God has taken me on to get me to the point of surrender and prayer, I realize there has been much molding, shaping, and purifying to prepare me. I hope it shows clearly as I shared my story throughout the book. I pray you are encouraged to seek the Lord and pray more.

My motto for twenty-five years has been "We Win!" People say it to me frequently after spending time with me, and I smile knowing the seed had taken root. When circumstances seem like you are not winning the battle, remember it's not your battle. It's the Lord's battle, and He's already won!

God is fighting the battle for you if you stand, intercede as a warrior with the sword of the spirit, and speak the Word of God as you pray. Yes, there are times when I still feel all those emotions I shared throughout this book, and I take it on as my battle, but it isn't mine!

Once I pause long enough to remember this fact, I release all the burdens of battle to the Lord, I experience His peace and I'm set free. As I stand and pray, God calls forth His army of angels to bring His will to fruition.

All of us experience such tests of our faith, and we learn to put our faith and trust in God, who will move on behalf of our prayers. Don't let the enemy bring on a spirit of discouragement when you don't see prayers answered in your timing. It requires trust and faith, believing God knows exactly when to work in a person's life. Consider the apostle Paul and the man of God he became in order to write two-thirds of the New Testament. I'll be the first to admit I don't want to experience the hardships of Paul's testimony.

He persecuted and allowed followers of Jesus to be stoned to death before he received his call on the road to Damascus. Look at the extraordinary work he did for God. I look at some of the people God has put on my heart to pray for...how messed-up events are happening in their lives. Yet, when salvation comes, and they are on fire for Christ, miracles happen! What a joy and honor to witness!

God gives assignments based on a believer's maturity, when we can see that it becomes less about us, and more about Him. Our vision and responsibility get bigger. Imagine the body of Christ as an army. You have privates, lieutenants, majors, sergeants, colonels, and generals, to name a few in the hierarchy.

A private's responsibility is much different than that of a general. A general is given the ability to see the big picture to lead, protect, and defend a large group of people. The generals are watchmen as prophets and intercessors, as they stand on top of the watchtower. God shows the watchmen things they wouldn't be able to see if they were fighting on the ground.

I think you would agree that if the body of Christ chose to unite together more in prayer, there would be significant change in the world. God asks us to step up and pray for His kingdom. When you consider the small victories God so graciously allows to happen in your life, can you imagine what it would be like for His church if we came before Him each day praying in unity as one voice? Many of satan's tactics would be destroyed. Imagine human trafficking being stopped around the globe. How about less violence and murder amongst our children?

I mentioned earlier the heart God has given me to pray for marriages and families. I believe when marriages become Christ centered, they endure the tough times and remain intact. It then flows to the children, as parents have a heart to nurture their children in a Christ-like manner. When Christ is the foundation, and at the center of relationships, all are based on LOVE. It becomes a ripple effect, but it has to start with one person willing to pray, because prayer is the weapon to win the battle, as noted in Ephesians 6:13,18 (NASB).

Therefore, take up the full armor of God, so that you will be able to resist in the evil day, and having done everything, to stand firm...With all prayer and petition pray at all times in the Spirit?

Pause for a moment and consider...are there instances where you have tried to move forward and fix things in your life before going to prayer and surrendering it to God? What if you decided to intentionally bring the issue to God in prayer for thirty days and see what changes take place?

What's the worst-case scenario? Maybe you don't see change and go back to where you started, but at least you tried and made the call to action. You might even see things get worse because the enemy you are fighting wants to destroy everything God is trying to do. Even though it is discouraging, it doesn't mean your prayers aren't working. The enemy is fighting against you to stop the fulfillment of God's promises. The call is for you to persevere through the battle and receive the breakthrough.

Imagine the recovery process of those fighting addictions and the battle during detoxification. It's not easy! It's painful! Yet, pain doesn't mean that healing isn't happening. God purges all of the junk.

95

The battle may rage, but your hope is in the Lord, and the promise He's given is "We win!"

The victory has already happened, you just have to choose to walk through the battlefield with God's guidance to attain your victory. I don't know how long that requires fighting on the battlefield. That's the tough part because most people want instant results. As the battle is fought, however, change is witnessed and hope is renewed. God reminds you that you are still moving forward and to persevere and intercede in prayer.

As I mentioned previously, when God woke me up at 4 a.m. and showed me the very reason for the pain and persecution I experienced, it was a battle cry to pray for others. The people to whom I ministered obeyed the call to pray. God moved and breakthroughs happened. Testimonies were shared of healing and reconciliation that brought God glory.

I urge you to start a journal during your prayer time. I recommend you begin by listing things you are grateful for. Ask the Holy Spirit to show you. It has helped me significantly through times of being overwhelmed. When I consider all the evil things happening in the world, the burden feels too heavy on my heart because I can't fix it. It's too big for me to figure out how to solve the problems.

I can't fix governments or stop terrorism, but I can stand in the battle of prayer, knowing God can and does take action as I intercede. Prayers become more fervent and bold as your belief and trust increases in Him. Putting a pen to paper and writing things you are grateful for reminds you of what God has already done, and it increases your faith and hope. As you go before God and pray for His kingdom, your doubts are removed.

As I meditated about the battle, God gave me a clearer picture of what His army looks like in a time of war. From a bird's eye view, I saw war was occurring across the land. I could see watchmen standing on the watchtower sending warnings and giving direction to the soldiers below. I saw myself on the ground fighting in the battle with the sword of the spirit, as I matured and obeyed the call to intercede for the body of Christ. I started on the front lines just as a private would during a war. I was against whatever individual enemy satan was using to attack me. As I won each battle, I moved away from the front lines and closer to the watchtower.

I was given responsibility to protect and train others. The battle became different. The enemy wasn't physically attacking me, as much as the people God had called me to train and equip. I saw that as soldiers matured and defeated the enemy on the battlefield, the more time they spent in prayer, just as I had been called to do…talk less and pray more.

As prayer warriors rose to lead and protect others, God provided a larger view of what was happening in the distance. It was necessary to see ahead to help others defeat the enemy. I saw people climbing the watchtower. They could see out in the distance what was happening on the battlefield. They shouted warnings and spoke the Word of God to help other soldiers. The watchman standing on the top of the watchtower could see for miles and sent forth words of prophecy and warnings to soldiers below. As those climbing the watchtower heard the watchman, they followed the directions given to prepare the soldiers on the battlefield. God showed me the most important weapon was prayer to defeat the enemy. Soldiers were speaking God's word, and as they did, the enemy crumbled.

Can you see it? I want you to imagine yourself on that battlefield. Are you on the front lines as a private, who is just getting to know God and fighting the enemy with a new set of armor? As you gain more knowledge of who you are in Christ, you enter the battle more boldly. Your faith and trust in the Lord increases, and you rest more in His assurance rather than your own strength. Your armor fits more securely, as you remember to always put on the full armor of God. As you fight those battles you become stronger, wiser and equipped for what is ahead. Your understanding becomes deeper, as the Lord brings you revelation. It's no longer just about your survival, but of those God has assigned you to lead and protect. In seeking the Lord, He shows you what they need, and your intercession moves God to intervene so they witness His power. Their hope is renewed and they keep fighting.

The key to remember is the battle is being fought in the spirit through prayer and not through your own strength. When you consider all the pieces of the armor of God, they are made for defense, to protect you from the enemy. The one exception is the sword of the Spirit. The sword is our offensive weapon to speak the Word of God. As you pray and call forth His Word, the enemy weakens, you gain victory, and God gets the glory. Prayer is the answer!

♥ Reflections

Are you feeling that nudge to pray more?

Where do you picture yourself on the battlefield?

Are you on the ground, climbing the watchtower, or on top of the watchtower?

Can you recall a time during the battle where God's power was apparent and increased your faith and hope?

What is God putting on your heart to pray for now?

Are you willing to commit to time in prayer for His kingdom?

Epilogue

I am overwhelmed with gratitude as I ponder my journey God has provided to complete this book. I was given a beautiful home in the mountains in a little town called Freedom at the end of summer through the autumn season. The house is located off a dirt road with beautiful flower gardens and old stonewalls. I walked out to the screened-in porch many mornings with my coffee in hand and ready to open my devotionals and spend time with my Lord. I heard the birds singing and felt the soft breeze as it blew by. I felt like I was experiencing a piece of Eden. The presence of His peace lured me to bask in His presence. It was quiet and still, and my heart wanted to listen and hear His voice. As He spoke, I wrote, I cried, I prayed, and I wrote some more until I completed what you have in your hand now.

I had those specific God moments that confirmed I was in the right place at the right time. The day I arrived there was a quick rain shower, and as the sun peaked out from the clouds again, double rainbows appeared over the home, a sign that God's promise has been fulfilled, and also add to that the name of the little town, FREEDOM.

I don't believe it was any accident that I happened to be out in the middle of nowhere in a place located off a dirt road. As I took time to go out for walks and look at the beautiful trees, the flowers, fields, and streams, I couldn't help but recall the dream I had walking down the dirt road with Jesus.

In the dream the flowers were in full bloom, as they would be in the summer time, and the grass was rich in its dark green color. Autumn is harvest season, and the beauty of the New England mountains is breathtaking, as they burst forth with color. I witnessed this beauty every day, as I looked out the window and walked along the road.

I had the dream in the Spring of 2004 and God has had me on a journey for nine years to produce this book in the Autumn season of 2013. There's a time to plant, a time to water, and a time to harvest. It's now harvest season.

I pray your relationship with our Father in heaven deepens as you seek Him. May you hunger and thirst for His righteousness (Matthew 5:6). May you experience His love and grace that stirs so greatly within you that it overflows to others.

I don't know where you see yourself right now, but I know God wants you to hold His hand, as you walk down your road and experience this life He planned for you, even before you were born (Psalm 139:13-14). God has a calling for your life that will bring Him glory and benefit the body of Christ. Don't let doubt and fear creep in, but push forth through the darkness with your armor securely placed, using the sword of the spirit (prayer) to move mountains. We Win!

Lesa Day, Thanksgiving, 2013

Jesus Dispels Doubt

"They were fearful and terrified...but Jesus said, "Why are you troubled?... It is I myself?" (Luke 24:37-38)

They had betrayed their Master. When Jesus needed them they scampered. And now they were having to deal with the shame.

Seeking forgiveness but not knowing where to look for it, the disciples came back. They gravitated to the same upper room that contained the sweet memories of broken bread and symbolic wine...

They came back. Each with a scrapbook full of memories and a thin thread of hope. Each knowing that it is all over, but in his heart hoping that the impossible will happen once more. 'If I had one more chance.'

And just when the gloom gets good and thick, just when their wishful thinking is falling victim to logic, just when someone says, 'How I'd give my immortal soul to see Him one more time," a familiar face walks through the wall.

"My, what an ending. Or, better said, what a beginning!" [xvi]

Acknowledgements

A tremendous team of people worked with me on this project. Some prayed for me continually while others read the manuscript and gave gut level, heart-to-heart feedback to help produce the finished product you have in your hands. Thank you to each of you and may the Lord continue to use you as a wonderful light for His kingdom.

Mark Wiggins – a man with a passion to make a difference in the world as a speaker and author himself and understands the power of team. Thank you for taking time out of your busy schedule to read and give honest, sincere feedback. I look forward to more collaboration with you in the future. http://moovin4ward.com

Dion Jordan – a man with a heart to truly touch people's lives. Dion has a sense of integrity that is exemplary and worth following. He inspires and challenges me to keep moving forward and go deeper to reach my full potential. He is "The Potentialist." He brings glory to God in the example he sets for all who know him. http://www.dionjordan.com/

Anthony Goulet – a man and dear friend who knows what's it's like to be out in the trenches every day. As a gang interventionist, Anthony knows what it's like to fight the spiritual battle and cry out to our Father in heaven for those lost and wounded souls. Thank you Tony for your heart and dedication to this book. You were a visionary who saw this project much bigger than I did and it wouldn't be the same without you. http://anthonygoulet.com

Julyn Farrington – my friend and dear sister in the Lord who is always there willing to help. Thank you for taking time out of your busy life to review the manuscript, pray, and encourage me along the way. I love you lady!

Lisa Lovejoy – my precious friend whose presence pours the love of Jesus each time I connect with you. Thank you for taking time to review and give heartfelt feedback to help me along the way. You are one of my greatest encouragers.

Theresa Robbins – A woman after God's own heart who went through each detail of the manuscript and shared the wisdom God showed you as you read each chapter. Thank you for setting the example of a grateful heart and a passion to serve Christ wholeheartedly.

Pat Davis, Donna Thompson, Anna Ziller and Marty Atherton – Dear friends, who have walked this dirt road with me for years through times of victory and heartache. You love me regardless of my flaws and give me insight to see the bigger picture. Your loyalty restores my hope to keep moving forward. I Love you!

Dottie Schmidt – A woman of God who's example to follow Christ empowers me to remain obedient to the call of God. Thank you for setting the example and investing your time in the project and interceding for me frequently.

Michael Charette, my cover artist and graphic designer enthusiastically offered to use his love for art to produce the cover. I love your enthusiasm and I'm grateful for your dedication to the project. Thank you Mike!

Dr. Caron Goode, my editor who made a heartfelt investment to draw out all the details and emotions of my journey, as I walked down this dirt road with Jesus. Thank you!

About the Author

Lesa Day

Lesa Day, an author, speaker, and coach has dedicated her life to serving Jesus for decades. Her prayer each day is to move by the leading of the Holy Spirit to bring God glory. She considers Atlanta, Georgia her home when she's not traveling for work or ministry. Visit Lesa's website at

www.pray-more.com

Facebook Page:

www.facebook.com/PrayMoretoGod

[i] Young, Sarah, *Jesus Calling*. (2004) Nashville, TN: Thomas Nelson (2004). Page 260.

[ii] Ibid. Page 302

[iii] Ibid. Page 211.

[iv] Blackaby, Henry, King, Claude V. *Experiencing God Workbook Edition*. (1990) Nashville, TN. Lifeway Christian Resources, 1990

[v] Young, Sarah, *Jesus Calling*. (2004) Nashville, TN: Thomas Nelson (2004) p. 267

[vi] Ibid. Page 259.

[vii] Ibid. Page 357

[viii] Curtis, Brenda. Reprinted with author's permission from https://www.facebook.com/brenda.curtiss?fref=ts

[ix] Glyn-Evans, W. "Overcoming Satan." *Daily With My Lord*. (Moody Bible Institute. (09-11-1979).

[x] Frangipane, Francis. *In Christ's Image Training..* https://www.facebook.com/francis.frangipane.9?fref=ts Reprinted with author's permission.

[xi] Reprinted by Permission, Glyn-Evan, W. "The Interceding Disciple." Daily with My Lord. (Moody Bible Institute) (08-03-1979)

[xii] Reprinted by Permission, Glyn-Evans, W. *"God's Tear Bottle,"* *Daily with My Lord*. (Moody Bible Institute) (10-12-1979)

[xiii] Kelfer Russell (1980) Reprinted by permission

[xiv] Reprinted by Permission, Lucado, Max. "A Raging Fire." *Grace for the Moment, Morning and Evening Devotional and Journal.Nashville, TN*. Thomas Nelson Publishing (2007) All Rights Reserved.

[xv] Reprinted by Permission, Glyn-Evans, W. "The Pain God Feels." *Daily With My Lord*. (Moody Bible Institute. (09-24-1979)

[xvi] Reprinted by Permission, Lucado, Max. "Jesus Dispels Doubt." *Grace for the Moment, Morning and Evening Devotional and Journal. Nashville, TN. Thomas Nelson Publishing* (10-09-2007). All Rights Reserved.